Poetic Reflections

Jennifer Mormilo

BookLeaf Publishing

India | USA | UK

Presentation by *BookLeaf Publishing*

Web: www.bookleafpub.com

E-mail: info@bookleafpub.com

ISBN: 9789360944858

First edition 2024

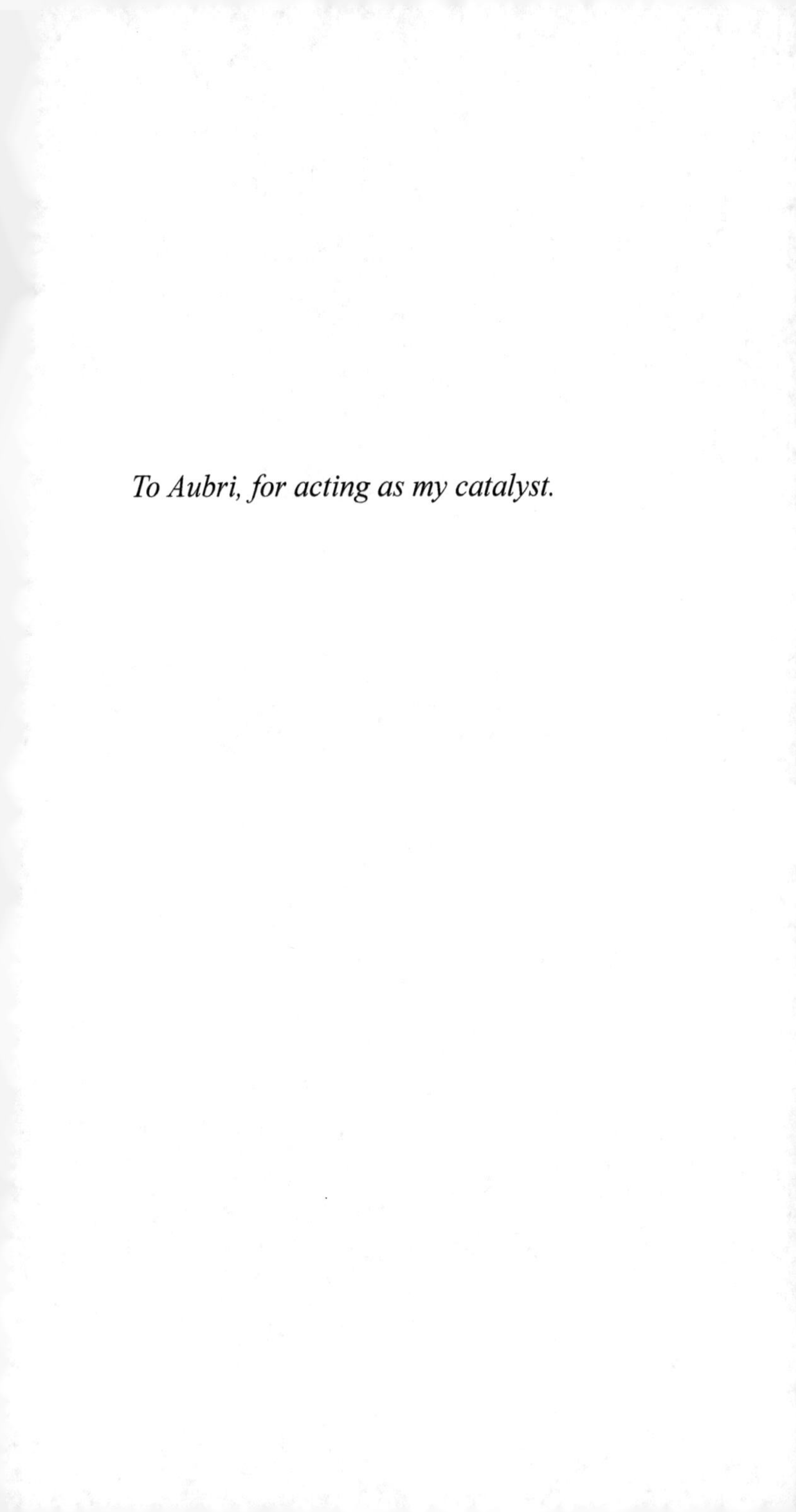

To Aubri, for acting as my catalyst.

An Unexpected Visit

We wake in the night, my mother and me,
To a sound heard afar from a source yet unseen.
Sitting up from the couch, feeling a bit shaken,
Questioning what to do next, both remaining
uncertain.
We tiptoe to the doorway and peek our heads
over,
Peering down the hallway toward a vast open
parlor.
Nothing of notice, so our hearts begin to beat
faster,
A thought crosses my mind, all else is then
shattered.

In a moment of certainty, I shout for my father.
And just as quick as the thought, his spirit comes
hither.
In seconds, he stands right before us in tears.
Sadness on his face, what seems to have pent up
for years.

His body looked healthy, and his hair freshly
cut, the best I've seen him in ages.
The scene that plays next is one for the pages.
He wraps his arms around me, a warm embrace.

He then sets me free, looking directly at my
mother's face.

"I'm sorry," he says, "Sorry for everything I've
ever done."
The look of acceptance on her face shone
brighter than the sun.

A soft sound was heard, what soon turned to
music.
My body awoke, the dream all but an illusion.
The message was clear, a visitation was reached.
I took that teaching forward, to help my mother
be at peace.

She reached her acceptance while he remained
alive,
But receiving those words, even from the
ethereal,
Was nothing short of a surprise.

We'll see you again, Dad, if only in our dreams.
Visitations are real, whatever real means.

Moment of Silence

My heart beats faster,
I feel a tightening in my chest,
A moment of unease encompasses me.

Mentally, I choose to be a step ahead.
In an instant, I place my feet down firmly,
grounding myself,
building strength within my being
while reducing my emotional reaction.

I navigate the moment before it can take over,
I recognize the triggers, both hers and mine.
I stand tall, with grace and poise,
Avoiding future regret from all the unneeded
noise
Of words I'd later wish I had never said,
Or thoughts that only I should have kept within
my head.
I found a way forward, a better ending too,
Taking a moment of silence before responding,
with finer feeling moments left to accrue.

Looking Inward

Meditation.
A space of stillness, where the mind unwinds.
Time, thoughts, and fears dissolve.
A soul's whispers are heard, unseen.
Here is where calmness resides.
A journey inward, to depths unknown.
Where peace and harmony are grown.
The silence guides us where eternity lies.

Misplaced Emotions

The air hangs over me with a chill.
I pull my jacket closer to my chest.
A man speaks loudly across the room;
my ears deafened to all other sounds.

My attention diverted as the AC blows harder
from a vent high above my leather seat.
A shiver runs up my spine, goosebumps down
my arms,
emotion crashing through me like a wave.

I look down at my hands as I write this—
cracks of dry skin galore.
My knuckles screaming out for hydration,
my heart and body sore.

Hundreds of people around me,
all moving through this vast place,
waiting to board, traveling to faraway lands,
the only semblance of sanity, seeing face after
face.

These emotions bubbling upwards,
I question sometimes if they're mine
or the feelings of all those around me,

struggling to be healed in due time.

This life is not made for the faint-hearted.
A wheel of death turned into light,
it's a choice to see one over the other,
many often leaning toward strife.

I open the front zip of my backpack,
pull out a tube of hand cream.
Slowly rubbing into the crevices of skin,
its results yet to be seen.

In an instant, I'm back in the moment, aware of
what appears all around.
This small step a part of my healing, and my
body homeward bound.

The Truth of Self

A new day emerges,
The sun's rays breaking through the clouds.
Its gentle warmth promises a fresh start and new
possibilities.
Moments of reinvention, leaving behind
yesterday's shadows.

Greet the morning with fresh eyes and fervent
strength.
Manifest your truest self.

I am Worthy

Look into the mirror,
A reflection you will see,
One with the universe
Vibration happening.
Embrace your inner worthiness,
Let it slowly form its roots,
Signals sent throughout the cosmos,
Aligning your pursuits.
Acting as a catalyst
To manifest your dreams,
Each step toward self-assuredness
Creates tangible realities.
Yes, you are capable,
You're more than worthy too,
This cosmic dance of reciprocity
Is the precipice for an extraordinary life being
built.

A Child's Insight

Unencumbered minds,
Surpassing our expectations,
Innocence and curiosity,
Remarkable intelligence.
Young children often overlooked,
Compared with adults,
Yet we must open our eyes
And seek out their untainted view.
Their profound wisdom comes from within,
Unbiased and without limits.
Let's respect this untouched intelligence,
Treating them as equals rather than inferior
beings.
Engage in meaningful dialogue,
Foster an environment of mutual respect,
Empower children to express themselves,
Honor the richness of their perspective.

Universal Connection

Twin flame, one and the same.
Two bodies, one soul.
Two minds of their own.
Two ways of working, and two ways of life.
But when brought together, ends all the strife.
Because two become one,
Yes, two bodies remain,
But what goes beyond is all for the gain.
The quest for shared truths, universal alignment.
It's all part of the grander plan led by our divine sidekicks.
Our guides push us forward, hold our hands when we need it.
Physical forms are unseen, but their presence is immanent.
Yes, our purpose is deep, stretched much farther than we see.
Our lives are not only our own, but the shared consciousness at be.
Two becomes one but one becomes so much more.
The truth of universal connectedness comes knocking at our door.
So, we must open our hearts, hear the knock getting louder.
We rise as a collective, let's make future generations prouder.

Yolk

Cracked open like an egg,
Yolk seeping from my pores.
Laid flat on a skillet,
Bare back against the floor.
Temperatures rising,
Liquid turning into solid.
My body overheating,
Life-changing forms.
A new purpose created,
Breaking free of what was.
Energy cycling.

Find Meaning in All Things

Life is a journey,
One we all go through.
Moments of self-reflection,
Coupled with moments of exploration and
becoming new.
Mingled with periods of uncertainty and
lingering feelings of self-doubt,
Reframing the experience opens us up to what
this is all about.
Partake in the simple pleasures like listening to
the birds sing,
Or putting together puzzle pieces,
Maybe even hearing the phone ring.
Sometimes purpose can emerge when we least
expect it to,
Building meaningful connections along our path
could be a good starting place for you.
There is no right or wrong direction,
It's what comes naturally.
Listen to your heart,
Be patient with yourself,
And remain open to all the possibilities.

Your Majesty

I peer out the window,
A haze shadowing the sky,
Below me, land for miles.
All appears silent from this height.
That, of course, is a deception.
A vast visual of bumps, curves, and cracks,
Mother nature's hands at work.
A closer look shows the results of our kind
clasping onto what came many moons before us.
A majestic sight: the browns, blues, greens, and
whites.
No string of words is sufficient to emulate the
magnitude I've become witness to.
So instead, I sit in silence of mouth and mind,
Forty thousand feet above.

Flower

Graced by its beauty as I gaze closely at its head,
Marveled by each petal, the delicate filament represents
A visual of nature human beings cannot deny,
Allured further by its significance,
Affecting all those far and wide.
This dainty little flower, a crucial role it often plays,
Of pollinating those around it, reproduction underway.
Nectar serves as sustenance,
A healing for birds and bees,
An intricate web of life,
Its fluidity like the breeze.
This flower might be tiny but its force symbolic too,
Evoking countless feelings of joy, love, and life renewed.

Magic Moments

A moment in time,
How fleeting.
A thought crosses my mind,
How fleeting.
One, two, three blinks of the eyes,
How fleeting.

Whisked off to a faraway land.
Not a single worry, my feet in the sand.
The sun shining bright, truly a delight.
And yet, this too, is fleeting.

You see, life is nothing more than pure presence,
And yet, most of us struggle to see it.
What's right there to see, appears more like a
dream,
But that's the sure magic we should believe in.

Within a Bubble

Light dances across its surface,
Refracting at its sides.
A shimmering orb of kaleidoscopic colors,
Mesmerizing to the naked eye.
A portal to another world,
Its iridescent depths.
Time stands still inside this bubble,
Its weight no depiction of its heft.
This world within a world brings childlike
wonder and awe,
A magical escape for one to emerge within,
Where anything is possible.

Inner Strength

Courage and conviction,
Two qualities you'll need,
To break the mold, defy the odds,
And all that's in between.
You want to be in movies,
You want to be on screen,
You're told those goals are lofty,
Are you seeking to be seen?
It's easy once you realize,
The power's all within your hands,
To liberate yourself from the shackles of the
land.
Remove those dirty habits that divide you from
your goal,
Stop those unwavering beliefs that leave you
sinking oh so low.
Step boldly into righteousness,
Look forward as you do,
One thought to keep you going is,
You are uniquely you.
There is no other like you,
No person that comes close.
With courage and conviction,
You will always do the most.
So, dream all your big dreams,

And fulfill all your desires,
Never let your mind keep you from reaching that
much higher.

Laws of the Universe

What are your intentions?
Do you truly know?
Do your beliefs shape your reality?
Is it your assumptions that dictate how things
go?
Or is it the power of the mind,
Your thoughts manifesting your desires,
Aligning with your emotions, leading you to
what transpires?
Could it be a combination,
Both essential to your flow,
Serving as the foundation for which your dreams
can ultimately grow?
Acknowledging both principles
Can lead you to success,
Harness the power of your beliefs and
intentions, and you'll be amazed at what comes
next.

Reincarnation

Echoes of past lives reverberate through the
corridors of my soul,
Shaping the course of my journey to this present
moment.
Each incarnation, a unique set of trials and
tribulations.
Wandering landscapes, obtaining wisdom,
Gathering gems along the way.
Experiences etched in the fabric of my being,
Sculpting the person I am today.
Through this morphed existence, I unravel the
mysteries of thyself and the interconnectedness
of all things.
Standing tall, a testament to the human spirit and
the boundless horizons forever to be seen.

Herd of Elephants

Bonds forged through familial ties,
Each member plays a role,
Within these traveling majestic herds,
Interconnection and empathy unfold.
Shared experiences form
The foundation of their society,
From nurturing matriarchs who guide the group
To protective bulls in charge of defending.
Communication flows through subtle gestures,
A deep understanding being born,
Cooperation at its baseline,
Compassion adorned.
Empathy and collaboration underscore their
community.
Humans can glean invaluable lessons from these
gentle giants at bay.
Despite our outward differences,
The essence is the same,
Regardless of the species,
The thread is not in vain,
To love and be loved is the purpose,
That binds us all as one,
When we coexist harmoniously,
Together we have won.

Unspoken Truths

I chose to put myself out there,
And open my heart,
To show the inner workings of my mind,
Often questioning if it even left a mark.

I wondered what the wall was,
That stood between us two.
Or how long it'd been forming,
Before our connection began to bloom.

I was given little pieces,
Just enough to keep me hooked.
But what I failed to see at first
Was that your pain dictated your behavior,
Which I justified and overlooked.

The truth started to unravel,
But the hook went deeper still.
My eyes opened a bit further,
And yet I remained stuck due to my will.

Time showed a fuller picture,
But each day made it harder to let go.
I wondered how we got there,
All the highs mixed with the lows.

I could see the stark contrast,
Your beauty mingled with despair.
Your fear and past experiences pushed you far
from a love so rare.

We never had a chance, did we,
With those walls of yours so high?
But the truth is I could see it,
See it all right through your eyes.

Separation now sits between us,
And I still wish you the best.
One day those walls will crumble,
With newfound strength protruding from your
chest.

Love is the almighty,
And must start from deep within.
When that lesson is one day realized,
A new life can begin.

The Truth Will Set You Free

Sit in silence for a moment,
Be right here with me.
What is it that surrounds you?
What is it that you see?
Do you hear the noises?
Or smell what's in the air?
Reality is shifting; beware.
Is it all objective or do opinions take flight,
And create a new perspective,
That shifts where all the light
Is shown on each surface,
Creating ones not even there?
What's once been verifiable,
Is now a bit unclear.
Truth is a unique concept,
It's hard to keep its shape.
Its complex nature and multifaceted essence,
nothing can equate
To coming even close to,
So, it stands beyond the rest,
A fundamental principle,
Guiding understanding, communication, and the
pursuit of happiness.

Death Seeps In

What happens when we die?
A question both profound and deep,
That lures you in, no matter your stance,
Pondered by philosophers, theologians, and most
everyone you'll meet.
It's likely crossed your mind as well,
Of all that must come next.
A myriad of beliefs and traditions,
Interpretation is half the quest.
It ranges from religious concepts,
Like standing upon Heaven's doors,
To finding solace in the afterlife,
While others view death as finite, nothing more.
Regardless of the truth that comes,
The mystery remains.
These questions only prompt us
To think further,
Feel more deeply,
Live every day and obtain
The common themes that connect us all,
No matter where we stand.

The purpose of life is so profound,
It's where interconnectedness begins.
So, reflect a little longer,

Heck, let it sink in too.
Mortality is just the face of another chapter we
only wish we truly knew.